Safari Animals™
Animales de safari™

ANTELOPE

ANTÍLOPES

Maddie Gibbs

Traducción al español: Eduardo Alamán

PowerKiDS press™
New York

Published in 2011 by The Rosen Publishing Group, Inc.
29 East 21st Street, New York, NY 10010

First Edition

Editor: Amelie von Zumbusch   Traducción al español: Eduardo Alamán
Layout Design: Greg Tucker

Photo Credits: Cover, pp. 7, 9, 11, 13, 15, 19 Shutterstock.com; p. 5 Anup Shah/Photodisc/Thinkstock; p. 17 Jupiterimages/Photos.com/Thinkstock; p. 21 Hemera/Thinkstock; p. 23 Tom Brakefield/Stockbyte/Thinkstock.

Library of Congress Cataloging-in-Publication Data
Gibbs, Maddie.
 [Antelope. Spanish & English]
 Antelope = Antilopes / by Maddie Gibbs. — 1st ed.
    p. cm. — (Safari animals = Animales de safari)
 Includes bibliographical references and index.
 ISBN 978-1-4488-3122-7 (library binding)
 1. Antelopes—Africa—Juvenile literature. I. Title. II. Title: Antilopes.
 QL737.U53G52518 2011
 599.64—dc22
                              2010024471

Manufactured in the United States of America

CPSIA Compliance Information: Batch #WW11PK: For Further Information contact Rosen Publishing, New York, New York at 1-800-237-9932

Web Sites: Due to the changing nature of Internet links, PowerKids Press has developed an online list of Web sites related to the subject of this book. This site is updated regularly. Please use this link to access the list:
www.powerkidslinks.com/safari/ante/

CONTENTS

CONTENIDO

Africa is home to more than 70 kinds of antelope. These antelope are gemsbok.

En África existen más de 70 tipos de antílopes. Estos antílopes se llaman gacelas órice.

5

Thomson's gazelles are another kind of antelope. They live on Africa's **grasslands**.

La gacela de thomson es otro tipo de antílope. Estas gacelas viven en las **praderas** de África.

Springbok, such as the one here, often live in Africa's deserts.

Las gacelas saltarinas, como ésta, viven comunmente en los desiertos de África.

9

This is an eland.
Eland are the largest
kind of antelope.

Éste es un eland
gigante. Los eland
son los antílopes
más grandes.

All male antelope have **horns**.
Some female antelope have
horns, too.

Los antílopes macho
tienen **cuernos**. Algunos
antílopes hembra también
tienen cuernos.

Male antelope use their horns to fight. They fight over land and females.

Los antílopes macho usan sus cuernos para pelear. Se pelean por comida y por las antílopes hembras.

15

Most antelope live in groups, called **herds**.

La mayoría de los antílopes viven en grupos llamados **manadas**.

17

Many antelope are good jumpers. Impalas can go 30 feet (9 m) in one jump!

Los antílopes son buenos saltando. ¡Los impalas pueden saltar hasta 30 pies (9 m) en un solo salto!

Baby antelope are called **calves**. Calves drink their mothers' milk.

Los bebés de antílope se llaman **becerros**. Los becerros beben leche de sus mamás.

21

Adult antelope, such as this gerenuk, eat plants.

Los antílopes adultos, como este gerenuk, comen plantas.

23

Words to Know / Palabras que debes saber

calf/(el) becerro

grasslands/(las) praderas

herd/(la) manada

horns/(los) cuernos

Index

Índice